# PRISON IN CHINA

# PRISON IN CHINA

A MEMOIR

ANN LIN

*atmosphere press*

© 2025 Ann Lin

Published by Atmosphere Press

Cover design by Felipe Betim

No part of this book may be reproduced without permission from the author except in brief quotations and in reviews.

Atmospherepress.com

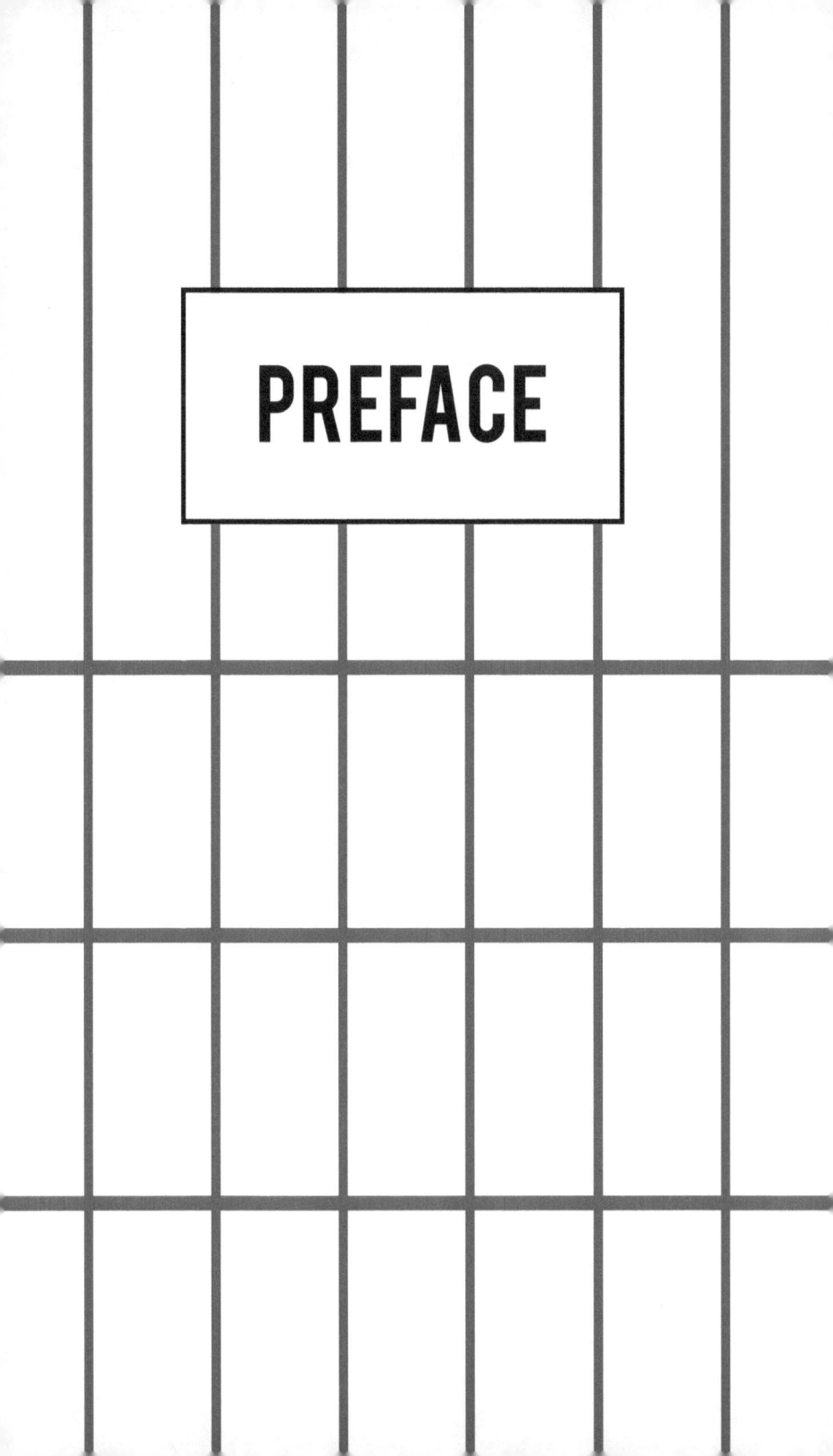

Hi, my name is Ann Lin and I am a girl from a Ukrainian village. My story begins in a poor family of rural workers. My parents never traveled out of the country and did not speak any foreign languages. My school years were spent in the local village school with a small number of students.

During my childhood, we didn't have an excess of money and my parents worked hard to build their own house. Despite the hardships, they always took care of me and didn't require me to work, being the only child in the family.

Most people think that adulthood begins after high school. But for me, it started in 2012, when I was only fifteen years old. One day, I saw an item on the internet that I really wanted to buy, but I didn't have the money. I decided to pick strawberries in the field to earn money to buy them. However, the money I earned was not enough. When I returned home, I promised myself I wouldn't labor in the fields like my parents and started looking for ways to make money without physical effort.

That's how I came up with the idea of reselling things online. I had no business plan, no money for initial investment, and no experience. That same day, I persuaded my mom to open a bank account since I was a minor. My mom supported me even though she didn't quite understand what I was going to do. The online sales industry was just starting to develop in Ukraine.

Two days after working in the field, I opened my first online clothing store. At first, it was just a social media page where I was looking for customers to jointly buy clothes from warehouses at a lower price with a commission for myself. I earned the money for the thing I wanted in just three days. I worked ten hours a day, communicating with suppliers and customers. I had to learn Russian to expand my services through communication with Russian-speaking people.

A few months later, I had connections with dozens of suppliers and hundreds of customers. I worked without rest every day and started getting a real paycheck for the first time. I had a lot of ideas and ambitions. My activity brought good money and my sales grew every month.

At the age of seventeen, I figured out a way to bring goods from China to Ukraine to expand the range of things. At that time, there was still no way to buy goods from China directly in Ukraine. I found a Chinese woman who spoke Russian and started ordering goods through her. I could afford to work from a button phone and travel around the country without restrictions. At that time, I was in school and dreamed of becoming a lawyer, but my parents didn't have the money for me to go to law school. I often skipped school while still working hard and studying for my final exams. With each new day, I looked more and more into my little business, which began to grow right before my eyes. I could not believe that I, an ordinary girl from a Ukrainian village with no experience or financial opportunities, grew up to be an entrepreneur capable of achieving her goals.

My friends and acquaintances marveled at how I was able to succeed so quickly and create my own business at such an early age. Some supported me, others looked at me skeptically, but no one could deny my resilience and perseverance.

As time went on, my online store began to bring in even more profit, and I could afford to develop it further. I started looking for new ways to attract customers, expand my product range, and improve my service.

Not everything was easy, of course. There were days when I struggled with hardships and setbacks. But I never gave up. Every mistake was a lesson for me, which helped me to become stronger and smarter. My efforts were not in vain. Each year, my business continued to grow, bringing in more clients and giving me more satisfaction. I felt that I was doing something important and useful by helping people find quality products at affordable prices.

At the age of seventeen, I received a state scholarship to study at the National Law University of Ukraine—it was my longtime dream. Suddenly, new horizons of opportunities and prospects opened up in front of me. However, with that came the challenge of living independently in another city. It was a period of real challenge and growth.

Moving to a new city meant that I had to be my own boss. I had to learn to manage my time, balance my studies and business, and make important decisions on my own. But I was ready for the challenge.

As a student at the best law school in the country, I realized that this was just the beginning of my journey. Having my own business, I found a unique opportunity to apply my knowledge and skills in real life. My studies became an integral part of my entrepreneurial journey, and I strove to use every lesson I learned to make my business even stronger. Every day I felt my knowledge and professional skills grow and help me expand my business. This experience not only shaped me as an entrepreneur, but also inspired me to strive for new heights in my career and life. The three years I spent at the university became real golden years for me. I was young, energized, and ready to conquer the world. Those years transformed me not only into a legal professional, but also into an adult ready to live and work independently.

At university, I made many friends, obtained mentors, and met like-minded people. We overcame the difficulties of our studies together, shared our dreams and ambitions, and inspired each other to chase new achievements. Every day brought new discoveries, challenges, and opportunities for growth.

My youth, ability to learn, and desire to succeed gave me confidence that my future would be bright and successful. I saw wide horizons of career growth and professional development in front of me. Every day I felt that I was moving forward, striving for my goals and dreams.

These three years were marked not only by studies, but also by many bright impressions, new acquaintances, and unforgettable moments. I believe it was these years that provided the foundation for my future success and happiness.

Despite the bright moments, there were also difficult times in my life. Although the war in Ukraine officially began in February 2022, its shadows existed during a much earlier period, starting in 2014, when I was just finishing school and preparing for university. My student years and the development of my business coincided with the period of economic crisis that engulfed the country. Prices for goods and services were rising every month, the exchange rate of the national currency was steadily deteriorating, and the standard of living was rapidly declining. In such conditions, the competition in the online sales market became more and more fierce and unpredictable. However, I was determined not to give up in the face of hardship.

In order to maintain my business and provide for myself and my family, I decided to expand my product range. By opening a sex shop and promoting other online stores on social media, I sought to diversify my sources of income and adapt to the changes in the market. All my efforts and labor were not in vain. However, despite my persistence and dedication, in the third year after the war started, I already felt that I did not have the same earning opportunities as before. Nevertheless, I did not lose hope and looked for new ways to achieve success and prosperity.

This difficult situation was further complicated by the fact that my mother was facing serious health problems. She required regular check-ups and medications, which were costly. My business could not provide enough money to cover all my expenses, and my parents did not have extra money. At the same time, my best friend went to work in China, which seemed like the perfect solution to my financial problems. Realizing that I needed to take financial responsibility for my family, I determined that the only way out was to look for new income opportunities. Without giving it much thought, I decided to go to China to work. Despite my fear of the unknown and separation from my family, I knew this was the only way I could help provide for my family and afford medical care for my mom.

Sometimes, when I talk about my life before I came to China, I feel like the words of the story refer to someone else, not me. It's as if it was in another life or another century. I remember myself as a young, confident, and ambitious girl. Until my early twenties, I never thought of myself as beautiful. I was overweight, had black hair dyed an unnatural shade, and valued my mind more than my looks. I thought I was unlucky with my appearance and couldn't love myself for who I was. This period of my life made me realize that our perception of ourselves is often shaped by our complexes and emotions, and can differ greatly from how other people see us.

However, China has changed me so much that I feel like my life has been divided into a "before" and an "after." I am no longer the young, ambitious girl I used to be, and this is evident when I look back on my journey. Each stage of this journey brought new experiences and lessons into my life, changing me as a person.

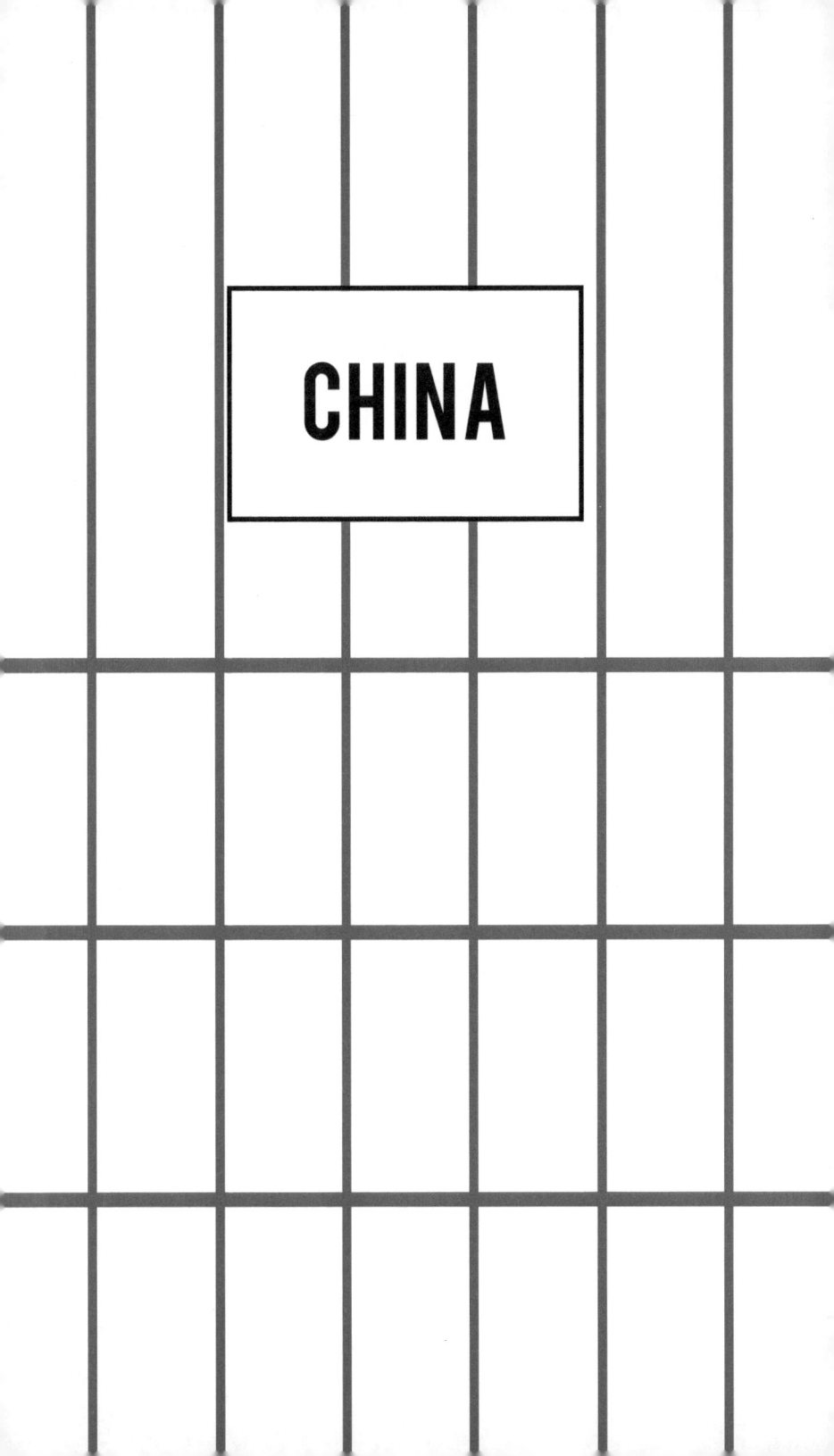

The dream of visiting China has always lived in me, especially after I started working with the Chinese. Despite many years of experience working with this culture, I had never had the opportunity to travel abroad, so as soon as the opportunity arose, I accepted it without a second thought.

I clearly remember my first flight to China. It was something incredible, the fulfillment of a long-held dream—especially since I was flying with my best friend, which couldn't have been better. But what left an even bigger impression on me was the moment when I stepped out of the airport in Guangzhou for the first time and saw the palm trees. It was such a thrill! Since childhood, I had dreamed of living in a place where palm trees were commonplace, and at that moment I felt that my dream was starting to come true.

I was full of energy and enthusiasm, not realizing how it would all turn out for us in the end.

That year, many foreigners—particularly from Ukraine due to the economic problems—migrated to China to work as English teachers, models, or nightclub hostesses. Interestingly, this work simply required being a white person. This phenomenon can be called a kind of reverse side of racism in Asian society: if you are a white person, you are considered automatically worthy of privileges and a special status.

Many people may be surprised to learn that racism exists outside of America and is not solely directed at dark-skinned people. In fact, much of Asia harbors racist prejudice against white people. I will talk more about this later.

Initially, my friend and I got tourist visas to enter the country. Our boss promised that later we would get work permits.

When we arrived to work in a nightclub, the task seemed straightforward: spend time in a nightclub or karaoke venue every night socializing with the guests. However, the culture shock I experienced left a negative mark on my soul forever. In China, people are willing to pay a large amount of money for simply being in the same room with Western guests, and even more so to be at the same table. This causes them to not only experience pride and excitement, but also, at times, to indulge in inappropriate behavior. I remember my shock when I first saw the rage in the eyes of the Chinese people who started calling their friends, pointing fingers at me, taking pictures of me, and touching my hands without my consent. It was happening everywhere—not only at work, but also on the streets and in the stores.

At first, I felt a sense of special importance and privilege, but it became more intimidating every day. It is nice to hear constant compliments about your appearance. However, it is scary to feel the stares of a group of men with inappropriate intentions when they start shouting obscene suggestions in a store. Or when people in public places try to violate your personal boundaries by trying to touch you. My friend and I didn't feel safe anywhere, and it severely undermined our morale.

One particular situation in a bank will forever remain in my memory. After all, a bank is a public institution where security and guards are expected. But when we went to change money, the bank employee froze in shock at the sight of white people and, naturally, did not know what to do with us. We spent a great deal of time waiting in line at the ticket office, answering obscure questions and filling out paperwork. After forty minutes, people started gathering around and shouting wildly. We couldn't understand what they were saying, but it was obvious that they were annoyed. Someone started smoking, others just shouted and waved their hands, and some laughed and filmed us on their phones. The situation became more and more tense as this frenzied crowd approached us and we had to run. The guards just watched and laughed at us. It was horrible and very scary.

I remember one time we were on a train to another city. My friend was asleep and woke up to kids filming her on her phone and screaming while their mother just watched and laughed.

There have been many similar situations. After all, Chinese society in general is not accepting of foreigners. To put it bluntly, they don't consider foreigners to be human beings. This is expressed not only in their behavior toward foreigners, but also in the laws of the country, according to which, if you don't have a Chinese passport, you have no right to anything.

The second part of my shock pertained to the culture—or, rather, the lack thereof.

In China, it is considered normal to slurp, spit under one's feet and other people's feet, and make all sorts of noises. After all, what is natural is not ugly. Smoking is allowed and accepted everywhere, even in elevators, schools, and hospitals. This contrast against my expectations and beliefs added to my culture shock and caused me to feel bewildered and disappointed.

Of course, we are talking about smaller cities, not like Beijing or Guangzhou. People in big cities are more cultured, but we lived in a small town.

I remember how every day at work became an ordeal—we

fought the fear of going and socializing with people daily. But we needed money and had no choice.

China amazed me with its beautiful nature and impressive megacities, something I hadn't seen before. I remember after receiving our first paycheck, my friend and I went on a shopping trip to Hong Kong. It was a huge accomplishment for us girls from the countryside in our twenties. We felt proud of ourselves, especially when we started helping our families by sending money home.

In my first days at work, I met Yang, who changed my life forever. He was an ordinary-looking Chinese man in his thirties. He saw me in the hallway of our nightclub and asked the staff to introduce him to me. We corresponded through a translator because he didn't speak English. He gave the impression of a very polite and intelligent young man. It turned out that he had come to his hometown for the weekend to visit his relatives and had organized a corporate party for his employees, but he didn't tell me what kind of business he was in.

We met Yang and his friends for lunch the next day. He showed us beautiful places and we started to see each other more often when he visited the city. I knew he liked me, but I was afraid of him. We had a language barrier and it was scary to trust people based on the realities of Chinese society. Yang understood this and tried to help us always. He took me to the hospital when my friend and I were sick, showed me beautiful places, and was always there for me. We didn't have any romantic relationship because the language barrier made it impossible. However, we spent a lot of time together and became really close friends.

In China, we had a good team at work. There were some girls from Ukraine, some from Georgia, and our boss and manager were Chinese. On weekends we cooked Ukrainian food at home and played games. Our boss often took us to restaurants and we socialized more as friends. I even told Yang that I considered my boss my friend. It gave us an opportunity not to despair because of the constant psychological and moral tension at work.

Around the same time, we met Sao, a middle-aged Chinese man who was like a father to us. He was very kind to us, often helping us if we needed it. He taught my best friend how to drive and often invited her to dinner with his friends.

Sao and Yang became really close friends and left us with many good memories. I will never forget how we went to pick tangerines in the field, go to the mountains, or take a train ride on the local river.

China is a splendor of mountains and valleys steeped in greenery and mist, beautiful rice terraces perched on mountainsides, and picturesque waterfalls enveloped in the breath of nature. Its cultural heritage is embodied in the majestic palaces, traditional temples, and intricate streets of old towns. The wonder of nature and the richness of culture make China a truly magical country. We were happy to see it all with our own eyes.

Two months later, as promised, our boss sent us to Hong Kong to change our visas to work visas. Our task was very simple: go to Hong Kong and hand the folder with the necessary documents to the agent, who would do everything himself. While waiting, we walked around the beautiful city and could not believe we were seeing it all with our own eyes. The power and grandeur of Hong Kong was a real delight. We had never before then seen such tall buildings and business centers.

Once we received our passports with new visas, we returned to mainland China.

After seeing all this beauty and finally making money, we were really happy in our twenties. I can confidently say that I was in love with China.

We originally intended to stay in the country for four months, but then our boss suggested we stay another month and go from Hunan Province to Wenzhou. It didn't take long for my best friend and I to agree. We wanted to see other Asian countries and decided to fly to Vietnam before moving to a new city. It was our first-ever independent trip. We stayed in a posh hotel on the beachfront of Da Nang and enjoyed the ocean view.

I remember the first time we saw the ocean and couldn't believe it. Two twenty-year-old girls from a Ukrainian village on the ocean—it seemed like a fairy tale to us. I remember the taste of fresh coconut that I always dreamed of tasting. After this trip, our life was divided into before and after.

On the last night in the hotel, I saw a small cockroach in our room. I have been very afraid of cockroaches since I was a child and I was very scared, but I didn't let it out and I didn't tell my best friend. I knew she was afraid of them too and I didn't want to upset her. The whole night, I couldn't sleep because I was afraid, but I pretended to sleep so as not to wake up my best friend. In the morning, we woke up and went to the airport. I was very tired and at the airport I told her that I didn't sleep all night and why. It turned out that she saw a cockroach too and she didn't tell me either so as not to upset me. She, too, didn't sleep the whole night but pretended to in order to let me sleep. At that moment, I realized I was lucky to have a best friend in my life. We have been together since we were eleven years old, we know everything about each other, and we love each other like part of the family. I think that not all people know how to be friends and not all people in life are lucky to meet a real friend. In this respect, I am very happy and that is why this book is dedicated to my best friend Elsa.

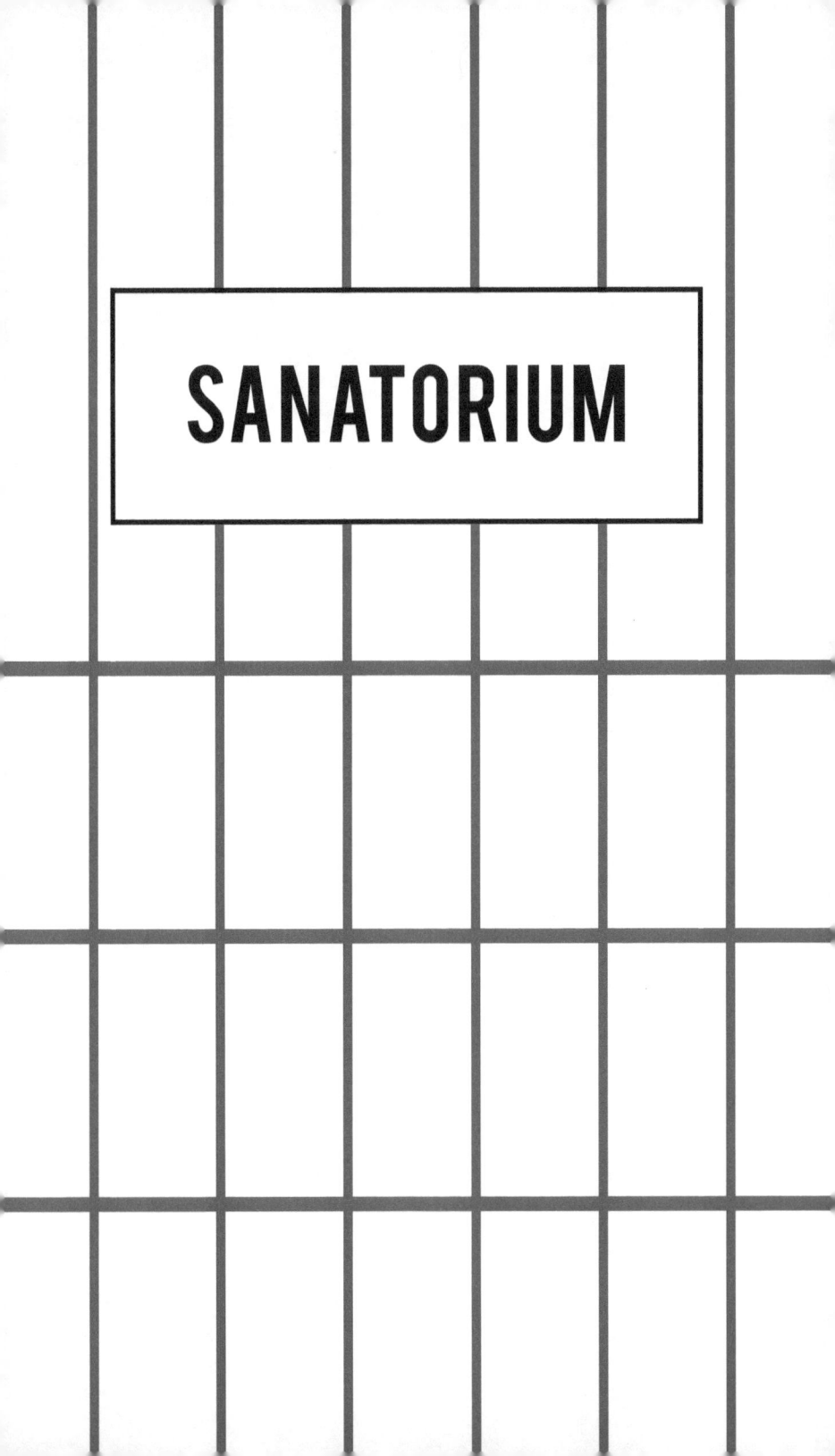

We returned from Vietnam to Hong Kong, got new visas, and, after gathering our last strength, we went to work for the last month in a new city, Wenzhou. The change of workplace was really stressful for us. We comforted ourselves with the fact that at the end of the month it would finally be over and we would fly home. We sent all the money we earned to our families, sent all our stuff by post to Ukraine, and bought tickets to Paris. We had never been to Western Europe and were excited about the upcoming trip and looking forward to going home. We missed our families very much and were very tired of China and especially of the people. Communicating with hateful people was a daily moral violence on us. When someone looks at you with loathing in their eyes like you're an animal, it is very scary.

The first week of work in the new city had passed and we were counting the days until we returned home. It was February 5th and we were eighteen days away from going home. We went to work as usual, where all the foreign girls were asked by the manager to go to a separate room. A group of men came in after us and closed the door behind them, not giving anyone a chance to get out. They immediately showed me papers and it turned out they were the police.

I wasn't scared because we had seen the police many times.

If our documents were in order, there was no reason to worry. The police did not ask anything, and after twenty minutes of silence, they took us all by the hands, led us out of the room, and forcibly put us in a car. It was winter and it was very cold. We asked to be allowed to take our outer clothes, but they ignored us and did not answer any questions. We were taken to the police station and again locked in a cold room. The female officers watched us and did not answer any questions. We asked for clothes and questioned what was going on, but we were ignored. At that moment, I felt scared for the first time. We didn't understand what was going on.

After a few hours of waiting in the cold room, an officer came in and started calling us one by one to another room. There were only thirteen of us—five from Ukraine and the rest from Thailand.

I went into the office and saw that there were many passports on the table, including mine. While we were kept in the cold room at the police station, the officers went to our hotel, into our room, and went through our things to find our passports. All this instead of just asking us to present our documents. Then we were made to sign some documents in Chinese without translation. They did not answer our questions and did not explain anything. That same night, they let us go home and of course did not return our passports. The next day, the police called our boss and told him that he had to pay a bribe to buy our passports for three thousand US dollars each.

After six days of waiting, we were told to go to the police station to get our passports. We arrived, and the officers gave us a friendly treat of delicious tea and cigarettes and smiled sweetly at us. Later, our boss arrived and put a bag of cash on the table. It was the first time I had ever seen so much money! The officers said, "The amount is too much, we need to count the money," and asked us to wait in another room. After two hours of waiting, a lot of policemen started to arrive. We did not understand what was going on. At some point, they told us to get off and forcibly put us all on a bus and started taking us somewhere. We were very scared. They did not answer any of our questions. When we got to a building with a high fence topped with barbed wire, we realized that it was a prison. All morning, the police had smiled sweetly at us, gave us tea, and, in the end, they took our boss's money and promised to return our passports. How could they send us to prison? And, most importantly, why?

The officers took our phones right away and made us sign documents in Chinese again. We asked in English how long we would there, but they didn't answer. I realized that I needed to inform my family, as they still didn't know anything.

On my knees, I asked an officer to give me a phone to call my parents. He gave me the phone for a couple of minutes. I called my dad and told him they had taken us to the police station and were taking our phones away. I asked them not to worry, even though I knew it was stupid. I still hoped for the best and didn't want to say the word "prison" so as not to scare them.

Later, we were taken one by one by female officers into a concrete room and forced to strip naked. At the time, I thought that was the worst part. I was an insecure girl of twenty years old and, for me, the experience was equal to rape. It was very scary, but there was no choice. We all realized that it was useless to resist because we were in prison.

All five of us girls from Ukraine were sent to one room, along with a Chinese woman who translated everything into English for us. The room was about ten meters square with a large, barred window. The view from the window was to the garden. Later, we saw men being taken there for a walk. But not us. Remember: foreigners are not people according to Chinese law.

There were six iron beds with mattresses in a row on the right. These mattresses smelled very bad, as though they hadn't been washed in years. To the left along the wall were plastic chairs that we sat on all day. The toilet was located in the corner of the room.

There was twenty-four-hour video surveillance in the cell. We were not allowed to sit on the bed during the whole day; we could only sit on the chair, walk around the cell, and talk. There was a TV on the wall under the ceiling, which was only turned on in the evening for two hours and on weekends in the morning.

We entered the prison on February 11th, 2018, just before Chinese New Year. In the first couple of weeks in prison, the police didn't come to us because it was the holidays and we still didn't understand why we were there. I remember hearing fireworks exploding almost every day.

Elsa and I were very scared. I remember the first few days; we spent the hours just trying to realize that this wasn't a dream and we were in prison. Just a short time ago, I had been in law school—how was I in jail now? And, more importantly, why? These questions kept us all on our toes. The scariest thing about this situation was the unknown.

After a few days, we got used to waking up to the seven a.m. wake-up call and folding our mattresses perfectly flat in ten minutes. We even learned our diet, which was very simple: rice porridge in the morning, soup and rice at lunch, and rice for dinner. No abundance—rice diet.

On weekdays, for two hours in the morning, we worked—we sat and folded iron screws. Next, we would put the screws in a box of newspapers and give it away. It really helped pass the time.

Just as the New Year holidays ended, the police started calling us in for questioning one by one. They asked how we came to China, where we worked, who our boss was, etc. We were finally told that we were in prison for illegal work.

They did not answer when we asked how long we had to stay in prison. They just said that the sooner we told them everything, the sooner we could go home.

I was jealous of our Chinese cellmate because she knew when she was going home.

Elsa and I were very worried about our families, so we figured out a way to send them a letter. At the next interrogation, we stole a pen and brought it to the room. When we handed over the work we had done, we pinched off a piece of newspaper. Since we knew when our cellmate was going home, we asked her to take the letter out. I remember us crying that night and tears dripping onto that piece of paper. We wrote that we were doing well and that we would be released soon. We asked the Chinese girl to put the letter in her underpants and memorize Elsa's brother's phone number in case the letter was taken during the search.

A couple of days later, she left, and there was no way to know if she succeeded in passing along our message.

We didn't have any clothes, as they had been left at the hotel, and we didn't know if we could get our stuff back. A few days later, our boss brought us warm suits and underwear for everyone. This was good news; finally we could change our clothes and underwear. But there was bad news, because it meant we would be in prison for a long time.

Everyone wore a prison bracelet on their arm. Inside it was a chip with our data on it. You could put money on it by name. Our boss put money down for us and we could buy hygiene products and extra food—eggs in a plastic bag, cookies, nuts, chicken feet, or milk in a bag. It was a real joy to eat something sweet. I remember the first time I felt hungry— not the specific physical hunger that comes from an empty stomach, but the hunger you start to feel when your body doesn't have enough vitamins or calories. Later, this feeling became chronic.

Our warden's name was Madam Wu. She was kind to us and tried to help us in every way possible—giving us clothes or pads and constantly asking how we were feeling or if we needed any help. We kept asking how long we were going to be there, but she said she didn't know. We asked her to take us outside, because we hadn't been off-camera for a couple of weeks, but the rules didn't allow it.

Not going outside for a long time is very hard mentally and physically.

Later, we realized that we were in the prison ward where people were held for administrative offenses, such as illegal work or drug use. Usually it was illegal aliens or Chinese people who were brought there.

On weekdays every evening, we had the TV on for two hours—our only entertainment—to watch a show called *Taiwan*. We didn't understand what they were talking about, but we were very interested. I didn't know what or where Taiwan was. All I knew was that it was some island in Asia.

Looking ahead, six years later, I will say that now I am writing this book sitting in one of the cafés in the center of Taipei City, the capital of Taiwan.

In the evenings, we often heard men from the top floor singing out the window. One day, one of our friends started yelling something back to this man, but we didn't understand what he was saying. Another evening, we saw a string in the window with a letter attached. Using a pen to pry it through the bars, we were able to get it out. The writing was in Chinese, of course, so we didn't understand anything. But the Chinese woman in our cell was able to read and translate it to us in English. The man's name was Yi Wen and he'd been in prison for a year and a half for drug use. He wrote that he was very sorry that the girls from Ukraine had been imprisoned in China. The Chinese woman helped us write a reply to him. We shouted out the window, he lowered down a string, we tied the letter to it, and he pulled it up.

In this way, we set up mail delivery between the floors of the prison, and every evening we waited for a letter from our new friend. He told us about himself and encouraged us in every way. He said wise things. He told us that prison was only a temporary ordeal that we had to overcome together. Once, he even asked his relatives to put some money in our account so that we could buy some food. We were very grateful to him. The officers saw all this through the security camera, but they didn't say anything. They often made concessions to us, even letting us exercise in the morning.

After a couple of weeks, I and another girl were moved to a neighboring cell. Elsa and I could not sit in the same room because we had to tell the police officers the truth and not communicate with each other. We thought that was very strange. Tell the truth about what? We told the whole truth. What else did they want to know?

It was my birthday at the end of March. I cried all day at the thought that I was twenty-one years old and sitting in prison in another country, not knowing when it would all end. Even more painful was the thought that I didn't know anything about my family. I didn't even know if they knew where I was, if they were looking for me. What did our friends think? What was going to happen next?

Elsa handed me a letter and cookies. She wrote that she loved me and missed me so much. Our new roommates, girls from Thailand, had been comforting me all day. Some had sick parents, some had children, but they all had one thing in common: they all needed money.

Looking ahead, I will say that after prison we became good friends. We live in different countries and visit each other every year. We trusted each other a lot and could always turn to each other for help. When you go through hardships with someone, even if they are strangers, it brings you very close together.

At the end of March, the police came every week and questioned Elsa and me. They asked the same thing every time—who made our visas in Hong Kong, what these people looked like, and who our boss was. We realized that we had some problems with visas, but the officers, as usual, did not explain anything or answer any questions. They came with an interpreter who knew ten words in Russian. We hardly understood anything he was saying. Just imagine the level of absurdity when the police couldn't even find a person who spoke English.

In April, the ambassador of our country came to us for the first time and we were allowed to talk to him for twenty minutes each. He said my parents contacted the embassy on the first day and they knew where I was. My father called them every day and asked if there was any news about our case, but the police didn't say anything to the embassy either. They had the right not to explain anything, because we were guests in their country, and by law the embassy couldn't help. The only thing they could do was find out if we were alive and if we had any health problems.

At the meeting with the consul, I really wanted to cry, but I restrained myself. I didn't want my parents to know how hard it was for me. I didn't want to upset them further. I said that I felt fine, that we were treated well, and that it would all be over soon, even though I didn't know when it would be over. I didn't even realize what was happening.

I remember feeling mentally and physically exhausted. We hadn't been outside for almost two months, hadn't eaten proper food, hadn't showered properly, and hadn't seen ourselves in the mirror.

On April 3rd, the police deported all the girls from Thailand, leaving only us five girls from Ukraine. We were still not told anything. After a week, Madam Wu came and took us to the room where all our belongings and suitcases from the hotel were. It was such a blessing to see my clothes.

I had my second cell phone in my suitcase. I remember when I took it out, I started to feel dizzy because I had forgotten how to use the phone. We even brushed our hair for the first time in two months and it was like an orgasm. We were told to pack our suitcases in fifteen minutes and to take our clothes to the cell to change because tomorrow we would go home. All five of us were moved to one room. It was our last night together.

The next morning, the officers came and picked up our friends. They said that Elsa and I would go home tomorrow because we had different types of visas. The two of us stayed in the prison room waiting for the next morning and made plans about what we would do when we finally got home.

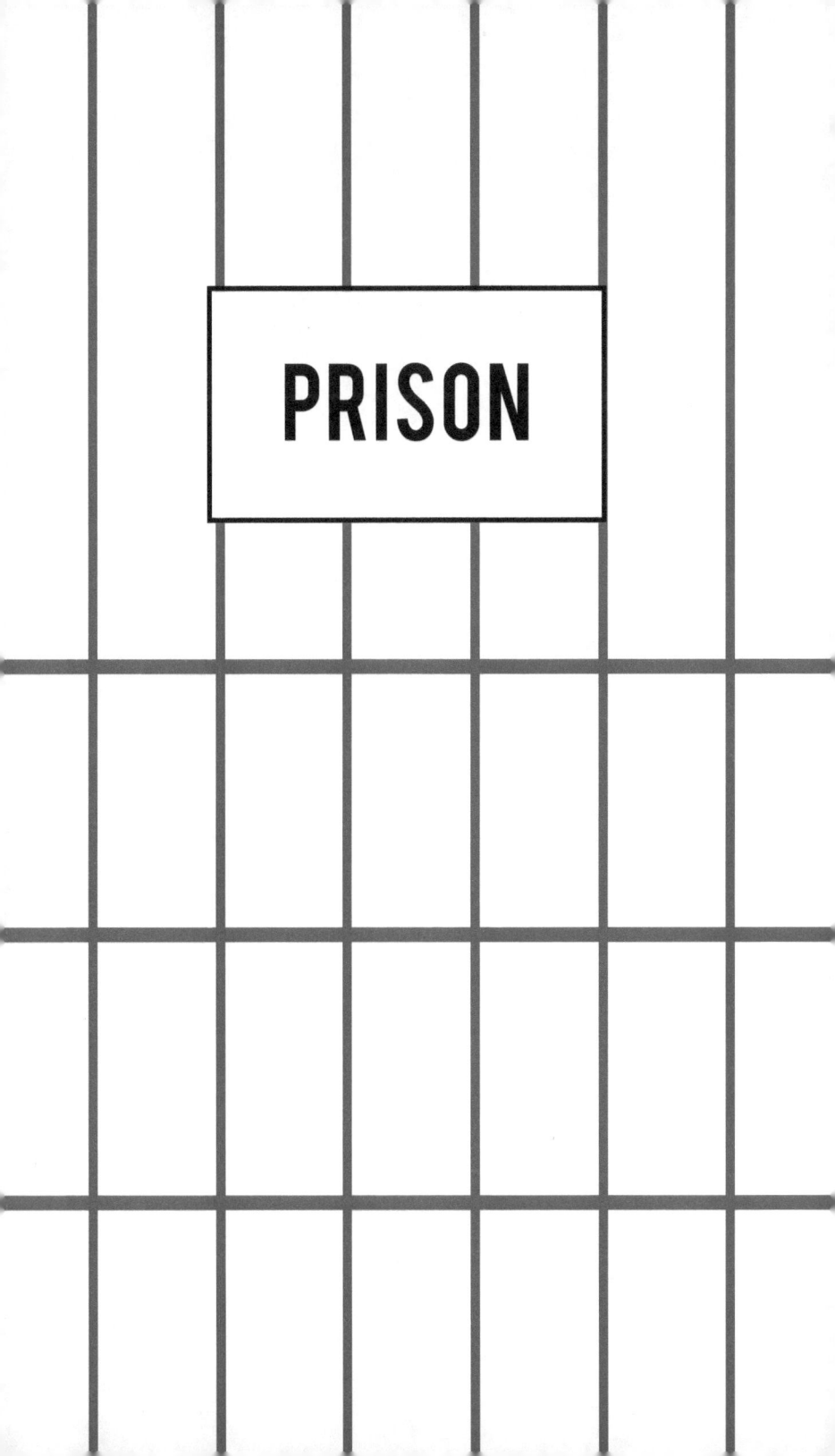

Elsa and I were picked up from the sanatorium, given our suitcases, and put on a bus. We thought we were going to the airport. We were brought to the police station again to sign papers in Chinese. Then they told us that we had broken the law, had visa problems, and were going to jail for another month. This was the first time they brought in a translator and said this in English. The interpreter was as impolite as possible with us and did not want to answer our questions. We didn't understand what was wrong with our visas.

I remember feeling so shocked and scared that I couldn't understand English. I remember being dizzy with fear. It was the first time I felt so scared, but unfortunately not the last time. I was so scared that I didn't understand where we were, what was happening, or what we were being told. We asked what was going on over and over again, but the officers still did not answer our questions. We were taken to the prison and saw the familiar walls—it was the place we had seen from the window in the sanatorium. The very place where criminals and murderers were kept. The very place where it was most frightening to go.

There are four kinds of prisons in China. The cruelest rules are in the remand prison, a type of prison where people are waiting for a court sentence. All the rules in this place are designed to make people suffer and confess their crimes as soon as possible. The whole system is designed to kill a person's personality. That's where they took us.

I remember kneeling and begging the policeman to let Elsa and me be in the same prison room, and he agreed. Now, years later, I think that's what saved my life. If I had gone through all this without my best friend, I think I would have died.

As soon as we were taken to the prison, they took away all our clothes and belongings again. We were forced to go into a concrete room, strip naked, and sit down three times. It was like being raped for the second time. We were given clothes and handcuffed for the first time. Then we were taken to the prison room, which was completely different from the room in the sanatorium. It was a real prison. It was noon, the hour when everyone slept. We saw people sleeping tightly in rows on blue mattresses. Fortunately, these mattresses didn't stink like in the sanatorium. It was a small room where eleven people slept in a row on an iron lift without pillows. There were two places prepared for me and Elsa. They took off our handcuffs and put on blue vests, each with a number. We were told to go to bed.

I felt like I was getting my second wind. It was like running a marathon on which your whole life depended. You run to the end with all your strength and then a new road opens up before you with challenges. You think you're going to die, but you decide to keep running until the end because your life depends on it.

At this point, Elsa said, "What if we're here for a few years? Look around, we're in a real prison." Soon, we were told we couldn't talk. We lay down on the mattresses and covered ourselves with a blanket. Under the blanket, we held hands because we were scared.

At that moment, everything was taken away from me—my life, my freedom, my belongings. The only thing I had was my best friend, with whom my whole life was connected, who knew me and everything about me.

Half an hour later, the bells sounded and that meant we had to get up. The Chinese girl next to us said in English that she would explain everything to us. Later it turned out that she was the only one in the whole prison who spoke English and that is why we were sent to the same room as her. She was asked to explain the rules of the prison to us. There was a woman in charge of the room who gave commands. On her command, we stood up and took two steps forward to the wall where there were low foam chairs. On her command, we turned around with our backs to the wall, and on her next command, we sat down. It later turned out that every movement in prison had to be done on command.

I had to learn all the prison slang in Chinese. In the prison cell, each person had a different duty every day. Two people cleaned the mattresses while everyone sat in chairs under the wall. These chairs were lower than usual and this was so that there was strain on the back and not on the legs. It was the third month in prison and sitting on these chairs made my back very sore.

Then, on command, we stood up, turned around, and, to the shouts of the prisoners "one-two-one," an iron door opened in the concrete wall and we went outside. It was the first time in over two months that we had been outside. It was a concrete courtyard with high walls and a grate instead of a ceiling. There was a washbasin in the corner and yellow lines under the walls. It was explained to us that we couldn't go beyond the yellow lines. We couldn't squat, raise our hands, or put our hands in our pockets. We couldn't touch other people. We could only walk and talk quietly.

Through the grate in the ceiling, we saw airplanes flying. Somewhere nearby was an airport. We looked at the sky and tried to realize that we were in prison, though we still did not fully understand the reason. It was the third month of our imprisonment and we still didn't know when it would all end.

In the real prison, we realized the sanatorium had been a vacation with friends. What was most frightening was the unknown. Not explaining anything to prisoners is a kind of moral abuse. Or was it moral violence only against us? Of course, we were foreigners. And this meant that we had no rights and the police could do whatever they wanted. All this time, the Ukrainian embassy was trying to find out something about our case. But the police wouldn't explain anything to them.

After the walk, we had dinner. The ration in prison was not very different from the ration in the sanatorium—rice three times a day. We ate from plastic boxes with plastic spoons. It was possible to buy additional food in bags, but we had no money.

Dinner was followed by a scheduled shower. Two people took a shower together in the allotted time—three minutes. The three prisoners on duty watched you during this time. It was a full shower for the first time in two months. We hadn't shaved our legs, combed our hair, or seen ourselves in the mirror for two months. I remember undressing for the first time that day and seeing myself naked all covered in hair. At that moment, three other people were looking at me besides Elsa. I remember the pain in our eyes when Elsa and I looked at each other. We felt so sorry for ourselves. For young, insecure girls of twenty-one years old, this was a very difficult experience. It took a huge toll on our self-esteem. We had to look at naked Chinese women, who don't grow hair on their legs. Compared to them, we felt like freaks and animals; we were different.

The next day, the warden came and asked how we were feeling. She was as polite and kind to us as possible. When leaving the prison room, a prisoner was always handcuffed. The two of us were handcuffed on one hand and led down a long hallway. Elsa and I looked at each other and realized that this was a moment we would remember forever. We were taken to the infirmary to have our blood drawn. Of course, they didn't want foreigners to die in a Chinese prison and instigate an international scandal.

For several hours a day, we sat motionless on an iron hoist (it was called a bed) in the lotus position. Physically it hurt a lot. My back hurt especially badly. Moving and talking were only allowed in the courtyard, where we could walk around for an hour a day. It was especially painful to sleep on iron bedding with no pillows. They made sure that during sleep we did not touch other people around us, turn over on our stomachs, or cover our faces with a blanket. If we accidentally covered our faces in our sleep, they would wake us up and fix our blankets. All the rules of the prison were designed for people to have no privacy, even when going to the toilet. Can you imagine how hard it is to go to the bathroom in front of other people? I remember how we couldn't go to the toilet for two weeks because of the psychological factor and we had to take laxative pills. Or how hard it was to stand and watch other people go to the bathroom. All this has a very strong impact on the human psyche.

After a couple of days, we were taken out of our room and taken to the wardens' work office. There was a telephone there. Our consul called us and asked what was going on. We said that we were in another prison and were not being told anything. He said he had been sent a letter saying that a criminal case had been opened against us for illegal border crossing and he did not know how long we would be in prison. Nothing was explained to him either. The not knowing was the most frightening part. Criminal case for what? What did we do?

A few days later, we were taken to interrogation for the first time. First, they handcuffed us in the cell, then they took us to another building. All the doors were opened only to the image of the warden's face. Everywhere we had to put our bracelets on a sensor to mark our passage to another cell block. I remember the first time I was led down a corridor, I saw men from single cells looking at me with evil eyes. These were men who behaved inappropriately in the general cells and were kept in cages separately. They were restrained with iron sticks—not beaten, just held. I saw men with shackles on their legs and I was very scared. I realized that these were real criminals and murderers and I was among them. I walked with unshaven legs and a bundle on my head and they looked at me like I was an alien. When the men saw me, they threw themselves against the bars and the guards tried to subdue them. They were like wild animals.

I was handcuffed and taken to an interrogation room, where I was locked in an iron chair so that I could not move. There was an iron grille between me and the policemen. They asked me who had given me the visa and what these people looked like. I had already told them everything several times. Then they told me to sign documents in Chinese and I didn't understand anything that was written. I didn't know what I was signing. I only realized that it was useless to resist because I was in prison. After the first interrogation, I was taken to a concrete room with a large window and told to wait. A military man with a machine gun looked at me through the glass. I was very scared. My back was very sore. I gestured to him, asking if I could lie down on the floor. He nodded and I lay down. I remember lying handcuffed on the concrete floor and trying to keep myself from crying. I had to hold on for Elsa, for my family. I had to be strong and get through this.

From the window, I could see the palm tree at the entrance to the prison. I love palm trees. As I said before, I have dreamed since childhood of living in a country with palm trees. I looked at this palm tree and was happy to see the color green. I looked and thought that this was not how I had envisioned life in the land of palm trees. All my dreams, plans, goals, and ambitions had been shattered by these prison walls. I didn't know when it would all end; I didn't know anything about my family for almost three months; I didn't even fully understand why I was in prison. I didn't understand why we were going through this ordeal. All I knew was that I had my best friend and together we would get through this. There was no other choice.

For dinner, we were brought our boxes with rice, but mine and Elsa's were different from the others—we had meat. From that day on, we were always brought a separate menu for dinner with add-ons. It could be meat, rice, seafood, or vegetables. We do not know why the prison authorities decided to help us in this way. Most likely they just felt sorry for us. We also did not know who paid for it—the prison itself, our warden, or the police? The girls in the cell hadn't seen proper food for two years. We really wanted to help them, so we gave half of our portions to them because they were so kind to us.

Still, we didn't have enough vitamins. I'll never forget that feeling of hunger. It's a different kind of hunger that happens when you don't get enough substances in your body. At the time, I thought that when I got home, I would eat everything and be happy just from that. But I was wrong.

In the evenings, sitting in lotus position, we watched television for two hours a day and were allowed to write in a notebook. Elsa and I couldn't talk, but we wrote letters to each other. One day, she wrote that there were two of us and we had only one problem—that is, we each had only half a problem. She also wrote that every day in jail is a step home. We don't know how many of those steps there will be, but together we will definitely make it. We tried to be optimistic and hold on for each other.

We wore rubber flip-flops and discovered we could write

something on them. We wrote *"home soon."* Every night, we wrote letters to each other with encouraging phrases and were happy when the date changed on the TV screen.

When we went for a walk, we often remembered our acquaintances and friends, our families, our school years, funny situations from the past. Very often we laughed at each other's jokes, no matter how hard it was for us. We even made up funny phrases, imagining what our friends would say if they saw us now with unshaven legs. We laughed a lot and constantly found reasons to smile.

People often ask me how we got through it all. I answer that we simply had no choice. A person can get used to absolutely everything and adapt to any situation. We appreciate what we have only when we lose it. In prison, we lost the most important thing—our freedom. Our families, our belongings, our time, and even some of our health were taken from us. I realized that they could take everything from me, but they would not take me from myself. I remember realizing how much I wanted to live my life; how much I loved and valued my family. I was ready to give up everything in the world just to hear my parents' voices. We had lost everything and we began to appreciate it. I remember us talking about how all our problems seemed small in prison. All our worries about money or relationships with men were nothing compared to prison. Prison taught us once and for all to appreciate what we have. Prison taught us to never give up.

There were four different night shifts and the schedule was set by the wardens. Two prisoners were on duty for two and a half hours a night. For twenty minutes you had to walk around the cell and see that other people did not cover their faces with a blanket when they were sleeping, and did not raise their hands or touch other people. Then you had to mark your bracelet on the touch screen and stand in the red square in front of the toilet for the next twenty minutes. If someone got up and went to the toilet, you had to watch that person. While on duty, you couldn't raise your hands, fold your arms across your chest, hide your hands in your pockets, or sit down. When your body gets used to sleeping on a schedule, it is very hard to get up and watch other people sleep.

I only liked duty because I could see the date change on the screen at midnight. It always made me happy because the new date was another step home. The wardens used the duty schedule as a way to punish the inmates. If you didn't listen to commands or shared food with someone, you would have duty every night. It's especially hard when your back hurts all the time.

I remember, once, a woman pretended to be sick and fell to the floor. No one believed her or reacted. She broke the rules and was punished. She was put in iron shackles so she couldn't move. She couldn't shower for two weeks, and to go to the bathroom she crawled on her back. She slept on the concrete floor. One night, I was on duty right above her head. She looked up at me, shackled in iron chains, and asked me to give her a drink of water. I couldn't do it by the book, so I just stood there looking at her. She had angry, hateful eyes. She was the only person in our room with such evil eyes. In all the others, we saw only kindness. All these girls went to prison for different reasons. Some sold information while working for a company. Some didn't pay taxes. Some cheated other people because they needed money to feed their kids.

People ask me if there is sex in prison. Or did you want to have sex in prison? My answer is no. You can't have sex, at least not in this particular detention center in China. You're watched twenty-four hours a day. Other inmates are watching, cameras are filming from every angle, and the wardens are watching from the balcony. Do you feel like having sex? No. We hadn't had a period in months because of the stress. Stress and constant malnutrition cause the skin to deteriorate. The body lacks vitamins and is constantly hungry. Because of this, the focus is only on surviving. I didn't want to have sex at all.

We continued to be taken for interrogations all the time. It was the third month in prison and we didn't know when it would all end. The police didn't say anything. I think they felt sorry for us too. I realized that this was their job and we were just names on paper to them. During interrogations, they repeated the same questions. Sometimes they didn't ask anything. They just told me to sign documents in Chinese. When I asked what it said, they said it said what I said it said. But this time I didn't say anything. We only understood that they were looking for the people who made visas for us in Hong Kong, because one day they showed us a picture of this woman and asked if it was her.

The policemen brought us cigarettes and allowed us to smoke during interrogations. I couldn't help but be happy about that. I tried to control myself and not feel negative emotions as much as possible. I realized that if I got angry and hated them, it would only be worse for me.

We counted every day we spent in prison. It was day number 100. One hundred days we'd been in prison. One hundred days of not knowing anything about our families, one hundred days of not seeing ourselves in the mirror. One hundred days of moral anguish and pain. One hundred days since we learned that mental pain is much worse than physical pain. For us, every day in prison was an ordeal, but we found the strength to smile and be happy that we were one day closer to the end.

One day, we were eating rice with plastic spoons for lunch when the door of the room opened. The wardens came in with a camera and brought us a cake. We were totally confused. They did not explain anything but said that this cake was for us and they had to take a photo with us. It sounded absurd.

They bought us a cake just to take a picture with us. We asked them if they knew that today was the hundredth day that we were in prison. They said no and we realized that this cake was a coincidence. We decided it was a sign that we wouldn't be in prison for 200 days. When things are hard and we want to believe in the best, we see signs in everything. This is how the human psyche works—even in the most difficult situations, we strive to see something good and believe in the best.

In May, the consul came to visit us again. As usual, I tried not to cry when talking to him. I didn't want him to tell my parents that I was crying. I didn't want to seem weak. He told us that we were going to be tried and we needed lawyers. The Ukrainian embassy had already sent a written request to provide us with free lawyers and we just had to wait for a meeting with them. On the one hand, all the court terminology sounded very scary. The feeling of fear had become permanent for us. On the other hand, as a lawyer, I realized that they would not let us go without a trial and it was part of the bureaucracy. I still did not understand—what had we done?

That same month, a lawyer came to visit us with an interpreter. Our lawyers were two young Chinese women. We were called in for questioning one by one. They explained that we had violated the border crossing law. We had a business visa but no business and this was considered a criminal offense in China. The penalty was up to one year in jail at the judge's discretion. The lawyer also explained that the police were looking for the people who made our visas. We had to identify them and that was why they were stalling. We were advised to plead guilty in court because it would mitigate the punishment and they believed we would be released sooner. I remember feeling relieved when I heard that. I mean, a year tops! Elsa and I could make plans for our lives starting the following February.

After the meeting with the lawyers, they sent the materials of our case to our cell. Everything was in Chinese and of course we could not read anything. The girls in our room read it and were very surprised. Later they told us that they thought we were prostitutes.

Elsa and I often made up nicknames for other prisoners because we couldn't remember Chinese names. There was one woman we called Fox because she had plastic surgery and her nose was too long. She was with us in the sanatorium for five days, then we met in prison in the same cell. She told everyone we were prostitutes, when in fact *she* was a prostitute. For prostitution in China, you go to jail for a month; for visa problems, it's a year. Where's the justice?

So all the girls thought we were prostitutes and felt sorry for us. They were as kind as they could be to us. They always helped us, bought us food, gave us shorter shifts when we had to mop the floor of our cell or clean the toilet with a toothbrush. Of course, everyone treated each other without judgment—because everyone had committed some kind of crime, no one could judge each other.

Every day after lunch on live TV, someone from the prison announced why they were in prison. Every day we had to listen to the story of someone talking about his crime and repenting. It was designed to make other people confess their crimes too. You couldn't move or talk. You just had to sit and listen and then, in court, say you're guilty.

In the room, everything had to be done at the command of the head girl. Ours was Fanghui. She was a thirty-five-year-old Chinese woman, although she looked twenty-five. She had a cute smile like a rabbit and her hair was cut into a bob. She was from a very wealthy family. She had a husband and two children. She was put in jail for running an illegal business, not paying taxes, and making a lot of money. Chinese laws are very cruel to people who make a lot of money. That's why she was imprisoned for more than ten years. I remember how she wanted to communicate with us, so she started to learn

English diligently. I never once saw her cry. She also talked excitedly about how wonderful her children were and how much she loved them. It was hard to realize that she hadn't seen them for two years—visits with relatives were forbidden. Her lawyer filed a lawsuit for reconsideration of her case and she was waiting for the result. I marveled at her willpower and character. How she commanded everyone and organized all the processes in the room. I looked at her and I couldn't believe that she was going to spend so many years in prison.

Every morning, the iron door in the wall would open and we would go outside to the concrete room to march. It was a drill. We had to stand in formation and march to the shouts of "one-two-one do must do." At this time, the wardens would walk across the balcony and see who wasn't pulling their knee up high enough. This lasted twenty minutes, after which we would wash our laundry in plastic bowls. Usually someone would be taken away for questioning. This time, they took Elsa and me.

At the interrogation, it was business as usual—we signed documents without understanding anything, smoked a few cigarettes, and were taken to a waiting room. The officer allowed me to lie down on the floor. I was lying in handcuffs and thinking about the fact that we would be taken to court and how scary it would be. That's when they brought my best friend in. She lay down next to me and said she'd just seen Mo in the hallway. Mo was the woman who did our visas in Hong Kong. The police had detained her and brought her to our prison on the other side of the country. When Mo saw Elsa, she recognized her. She gestured to her handcuffed hands and nodded, implying that there was nothing she could do. We lay on the cold floor in handcuffs thinking that it was because of us that someone else was imprisoned. We felt guilty. In the evening, Elsa wrote me a letter saying that we shouldn't blame ourselves. After all, we didn't know what else this woman did.

Making visas for foreigners was her business and we didn't force her to do it. Moreover, we were victims of her activities and of our boss, who lied to us about making work permits.

In difficult situations, there's always someone to blame. Just not yourself. Sitting in prison, I realized that we young girls had committed a crime without knowing it. We were guilty, at least, of not checking the type of visa ourselves, and also for accepting illegal work and believing our boss. But we didn't deserve such a heavy punishment. You can blame someone, or you can accept the situation with all its consequences and draw conclusions for the future. Sometimes that can be very hard. It's especially hard when you feel it's unfair.

I remember the morning when I was questioned again before the court. I was signing some documents without understanding anything, only now with the prosecutor instead of the police. I was so tired of not understanding. The girls in our room could read books or watch TV in their own language. We envied them because we didn't understand anything and the only thing that saved us was that Elsa and I could write letters to each other.

After the interrogation, I lay in the concrete room under the officer's supervision and thought about how tired I was, mentally and physically. But I had no choice. I couldn't be weak in this situation. I decided that if my life made me start to understand this difficult language, I would not resist anymore. I decided that I would learn Chinese no matter how hard it was. Even if I was deported from China and never went back again, I would still find a place to use Chinese.

I realized learning Chinese under such circumstances was a good way to kill time. It was also a way to keep my brain sharp.

That night, I asked our Chinese friend to write me the Pinyin alphabet and basic words so that I could start learning. From that day on, I learned new words every day. My goal was to start understanding as soon as possible.

I remember going to bed and the Chinese girl would say "wan an" and I would realize it meant "good night."

We called this girl by her Ukrainian name, Vera. She was very sweet and kind to us. She had long, beautiful hair, which she soon cut short. Her husband was in the same prison. They were arrested together for scamming other Chinese people in a neighboring country and getting money from them. It was a very common activity and a lot of people went to jail for it.

Looking at her, it was hard to imagine that she was capable of deceiving other people. She said that she and her husband had two small children and they did it because they needed money. They were taken to jail from their home in the middle of the night and had to tell the children they were going on business. It was obvious that they had ruined their children's childhood because now they would spend it without their parents.

One day, Vera asked to go on TV to tell her story for the other inmates. She said she did it so that her husband could see her. She was not even able to give him a letter because it was forbidden. Looking at these people, we had mixed emotions. On the one hand, we knew they were the real criminals. But on the other hand, we felt sorry for them. Especially when they were all so kind to us. We felt that we were all human and we all made mistakes. We couldn't be surprised or condemn them for it. I guess it was prison that taught me to never judge other people. I realized that everyone has their own truth and there are reasons for everything.

The morning of July 24th came, the day of the trial. In the morning, the wardens came to pick us up. They handcuffed us as usual and took off our vests. They took us to another section of the prison and made us put shackles on our legs. The iron rings on the feet were tightened against the leg and pulled the tendons near the foot. It made it very painful to walk. It was done on purpose so that we didn't move around too much.

They put us in a barred car and took us to court. We saw the city for the first time in five months. We were shocked to see civilization. Our eyes weren't used to seeing anything but gray walls. We saw people on the streets—they were free. We were so jealous of them and believed that soon we would be released. Elsa and I were brought to the basement of the courthouse and told to get out of the car. We were chained together and each of us was held by the hands of two officers on both sides.

At that moment, I felt both sorry for us and amused at the same time. It was funny because we were being treated as especially terrible criminals and murderers. Since we already knew that we were in jail because of our visas, it added a special irony to the situation. At that moment, I thought, *What's the point of this circus? What can I do to you? Why chain me up and hold me on both sides? It's absurd.*

We were taken into the courthouse and put in separate cages. They were one-meter-square padded rooms with bars instead of doors. We sat in chains in these cages like animals in a zoo. The court workers started coming one by one to look at us and shouting to each other, "Go look, they are from Ukraine." It was disgusting. At that moment, I didn't feel human. That moment was deeply imprinted on my psyche. I still feel pain when I remember it.

Our consul and our lawyers were present at the court hearing. We finally had a normal interpreter who spoke in Russian. She translated every sentence for us. We took turns standing up and confessing that we had committed a terrible crime and that we regretted it. After that, we were taken out and sent back to the prison in the same barred car. We were not told how long we would be in prison or how long we would have to wait for the court sentence. We cried the whole evening because we were tired, humiliated, and were not told anything.

We were informed by our roommate, who translated everything into English for us, that we were the first foreigners to go to prison in this city. As it turned out, her lawyer was the boss of our free lawyers. He told her all about our case. He also said it was a new law that we were being convicted under. It had only gone into effect a couple of months prior. Imagine how lucky we were to be the first in a prison where people had never seen a foreigner. It was a one-in-a-billion case, I think.

After a couple of weeks of waiting, we were suddenly taken out of our room, cuffed in iron shackles, and sent somewhere in our favorite cage car. We realized we were going to court to hear our verdict. The judge said that we were sentenced to six months and fifteen days in jail, and were fined 300 dollars. We were happy to hear that. It meant we would be going home in two weeks.

As I've said before, the scariest part is the unknown. If we had known from day one that we would be in prison for half a year, it would have been much easier mentally. We would not have been so scared and nervous and there would not have been so many physical health consequences.

We rejoiced like children and made plans for the future. We thought that, in two weeks, all the difficulties in our lives would be over. But we were wrong; prison was just the beginning. Yes, it was the worst thing that happened in my life, but prison taught me that you have to fight all your life for a place on this earth. Prison taught me to accept injustice and to control my emotions. It was very painful for us to look at our Chinese friends who were so kind to us, because we knew that each of them would be in prison for several years. Some of them would be in prison for ten years or more. We looked at them and it was hard to believe it.

The morning of August 25th arrived—that was the day we

were to be deported. We stared at the clock all morning and did not even talk to each other. Elsa and I could not believe that today it would all end. I wanted to cry with fear and uncertainty.

At lunchtime, it was scheduled to be nap time. We all went to bed, but Elsa and I couldn't sleep. We just lay there looking at the clock and at each other. While we were sleeping, the door of our room opened and the wardens came to get us. We were told to take off our blue vests and come out. It was the first time we were not handcuffed. We came out and everyone was lying in a row, looking at us with tears in their eyes. It was so painful for us to leave and realize that we couldn't even hug all these girls goodbye. They were all like family to us. They'd all been good to us. And now we had to say goodbye with the realization that we would never see each other again in our lives.

# THE END AND THE BEGINNING

We were brought to the airport, accompanied by officers from the prison. They were dressed in civilian clothes, so it was unclear from the outside what was going on. They politely explained to us that we would receive our phones in Beijing, where we were now flying. We were allowed to go to the smoking room, where, for the first time in six months, I saw myself in the mirror. Overgrown eyebrows, problem skin, regrown hair...I looked awful. But in that moment, I realized that I liked myself. I felt like they took my looks from me and then gave them back. I know it sounds weird, but in that moment, I reevaluated myself and changed the way I felt about myself. I decided I was never going to consider myself ugly as I had before.

Beauty is a relative concept. Beauty comes from within, from loving yourself. I didn't have self-love or beauty before.

We flew to Beijing and had to wait a few hours for our plane to Ukraine. Our wardens took us to their hotel and allowed us to rest, take a shower, and sort out our belongings in our suitcases. Afterward, they invited us to a restaurant—the people who had controlled us in prison sat and ate at the same table with us. We couldn't believe it.

They said they were sorry for us—sorry it happened to us, that we didn't do anything wrong. It was just the laws of

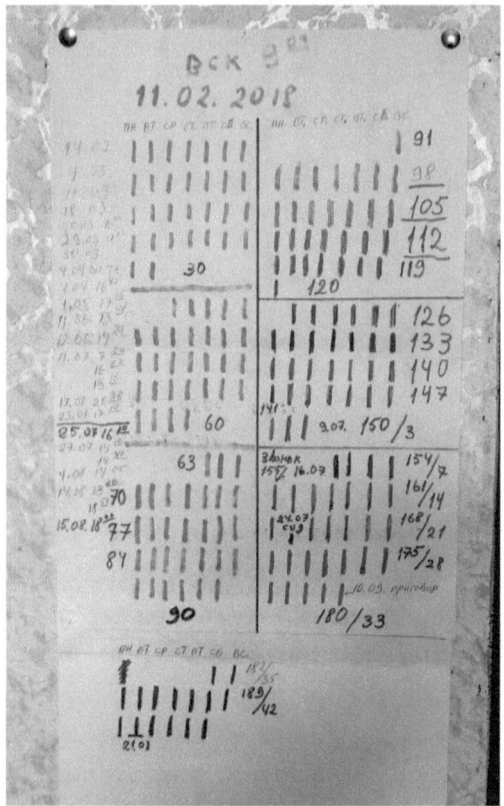

My father's calendar of the days I spent incarcerated

their country and their job. It's called humanity. If you ask me if I hate the Chinese for what they did to us, I would say no. I hate their communist regime and laws. But I don't hate the people. China is an example that laws are not people. A common regime in a country doesn't mean there is no humanity. At twenty years old, this fact broke a lot of stereotypes in my head.

At the airport, just before we boarded the plane, we were given cell phones so we could contact our families. It turned out that all my social media accounts had been deleted or blocked and I couldn't text anyone. We were able to contact Elsa's brother and he said he was on his way to the airport with my father. In Ukraine, the airport is seven hours away from our home, but our relatives couldn't wait to see us so much that they left for the airport much earlier.

Our wardens said goodbye to us. I realized that I would never visit China again in my life and got on the plane. We flew for nine hours and couldn't believe it was all over. We couldn't sleep from excitement, even though we were very tired. Lack of sleep is a normal reaction of the body to severe stress. I remember seeing young guys on an airplane talking rudely to stewardesses. It was a shock to me. I was not used to seeing people. The whole flight, I was just thinking that the most important thing in life was family and hoping my parents were okay. I was happy that I was alive and would soon see my family.

Our families met us at the airport. When I saw my father, I couldn't believe my eyes. It was the first time I had seen such a gaunt and grief-stricken man. His eyes were full of sadness and tears. It still hurts to think of it to this day.

I asked how my cousin was doing. She was pregnant. My father said that she gave birth to my nephew on July 24th and named him with my favorite male name, even though she didn't know it was my favorite name. How can you not believe in coincidences?

From the airport, we drove straight to the embassy to meet our consul, who, coincidentally, had also flown to Ukraine. We hugged and cried because it was all over. He admitted that he did not understand what had happened and that it was the first time in his practice he had seen Ukrainians being held in prison for such a long time without any explanation.

We drove home for seven hours and Elsa at some point stopped realizing where she was. She was very dizzy and scared. We had to stop for her to drink water and come to her senses. No one understood what was happening to her. It turned out it was her first panic attack, but we didn't know that yet.

All my relatives were waiting for me at home. I saw my mother and could not believe my eyes. She had lost weight, unable to eat because of constant nausea, and had no strength to get out of bed. She was heartbroken. And it was all because of me. I felt guilty and criminal.

I'd been told every day for half a year I'd committed a

crime and done something terrible. At home, however, I was shocked that no one thought that. It turned out that all my friends immediately noticed I had disappeared and contacted my family. The whole time, they were constantly calling my parents and asking if there was any news about us.

I felt as if I had died and come back to life. I really believed that everyone hated me because I was a criminal. But I didn't expect such a reaction from my friends. I have to thank them especially for their support. I don't think I could have done it without them. After all, people who have gone through such an experience always need support from family and friends.

I remember, in the first days home, it was painful for me to walk because some of the muscles in my legs had atrophied. My friends tried to visit me all the time and go for walks with me. They all noticed that I was not myself. It was very hard for me to get back to normal. It was especially hard to believe it was all over. It was hard to do everyday tasks. I remember how I couldn't go to the shower at first because I didn't have the strength for it and failed to realize that I could just get up and go to the shower alone.

The feeling of being deeply lost followed me everywhere. It was such a shock to be in the normal world. My brain just refused to understand what was happening. For the first couple of days, I couldn't sort out my things. I couldn't do anything on my own. I also didn't sleep for the first four days. I remember that feeling of being dizzy and tired, but still couldn't sleep because of the intense anxiety. In prison, I thought that when I got home I would eat everything, but the reality was I couldn't even look at the food. It all seemed tasteless to me. I couldn't eat anything. For the first month, my body was very swollen because I couldn't move properly. Daily I experienced physical and mental pain.

There is a theory that criminals who have been in prison

once will in most cases go back there again. From my experience, I can say that this is probably because once you have gone through the process of adapting to prison, you are no longer afraid to be there. It becomes the norm for you. Not being able to make your own decisions becomes familiar. It becomes hard to live in the real world, to make your own decisions and live among people. It is hard to live with constant feelings of shame and guilt. People who have lived through the prison experience constantly feel bad, inferior, or unworthy of a normal life. I think it is because of these feelings that the risk of relapse is greatly increased. A person at the subconscious level thinks that he has nothing to lose and it becomes easier to commit another crime.

In such cases, the support of others is very important. As I said, I was lucky to get support from family and friends. But a lot of people can't get that in the same situation. When we experience this kind of thing, we become very vulnerable and weak. The worst thing is that we think we are criminals. We think we are worse than other people and not worthy of living in a normal society. This is something you need to know if someone close to you has been to prison. It took me several years of psychotherapy to realize that I am worthy of living a normal life and being in the company of normal people. The belief that I was a criminal and not worthy of anything lived in me for several years. Only psychotherapy helped me to get rid of it. The only advice I would have given myself in the past is to start getting treatment earlier.

I remember the first couple of weeks home, my friend Yevhenii would come to my house and make me eat. I remember how hard it was for me. He always supported me and my family morally. We often went for walks in the forest, even though it was hard for me to even get out of bed. He literally forced me to go on walks with him. I remember that period of my life very badly. But I do remember telling Yevhenii one day that I had a hard time talking to people. I constantly felt like I was talking loudly. I know how weird that sounds. But it was real to me then.

He realized that something was wrong with me and asked me to go with him to the doctor. I agreed because I knew I needed help, but I didn't understand what was happening to me.

During that period, I also started to notice problems with my memory. I couldn't tell what I ate in the morning; I tried to read books and didn't understand anything. I felt sick all the time and had no energy. Yevhenii took me to another city to see a psychiatrist. When I told the doctor all my symptoms, he immediately diagnosed me with clinical depression and prescribed me antidepressants. I am grateful to my friend for his help—if not for him, I likely would not have gone to the doctor.

The worst thing about depression is the helplessness. Most of the time, people with depression don't realize they are depressed. It's like a gray abyss into which we sink deeper every day. It's a terrible disease that can take years off people's lives. I was fortunate to have a trusting relationship with a friend of mine who recognized right away that something was wrong with me. I truly feel sorry for people who don't have such a person in their life.

I was prescribed the weakest dose of antidepressant and sleeping pills. The pills improved my condition almost immediately. I was at least able to start eating and sleeping. But that was only the beginning of my long road to recovery. I also had a lot of health problems. My body swelled, and the muscles in my legs atrophied. I had problems with my skin and hair. Because of stress, the capillaries in one of my eyes ruptured and I could not see well. However, these are all small things compared to how this stress affected my parents' health.

My father started having heart and blood pressure problems. While I was in prison, he had a heart attack. My mother hardly got out of bed. She didn't eat anything and had no idea what was going on. It was very painful for me to look at her. I knew she needed help too, so my friend found a doctor for her. She was also depressed, but in a very severe form. Her condition was critical and she had to go to the hospital. I remember it all with horror, but at that time it seemed to me that the biggest horror in my life was already over. I remember how much I wanted to live and how happy I was to be alive. I think it was during that period that I started to appreciate life and everything I had. I realized that the most important thing in life was my family and my parents' health. I was ready to give everything to make them better.

I remember a couple of days after I got home, I called Yang for the first time and spoke to him in bad Chinese. It turns out he was looking for me. He'd found our boss and discovered we were in jail. But there was nothing he could do. Yang has his own big business in South China—an oil refinery. He told me about the corruption in that country. All businessmen have to pay the police to stay out of jail. He also told me that ten years ago he was in jail for months because he didn't want to pay the police. That's very scary. He was very supportive and saw how hard it was for me. He called every day and asked how I was feeling. He told me how sorry he was that this happened to us in his country. My mother was in the hospital and he fully paid for her treatment, for which I am very grateful. This act is another example of Chinese humanity.

Elsa had gone to stay with her family in Poland. She was as depressed as I was. It was just as difficult for her to get back to normal life. We stayed in touch and supported each other as much as we could. But we knew we both needed to be with our parents.

After returning home, I decided not to give up and to keep learning Chinese. I came up with a whole self-learning system. I watched YouTube videos every day, learning how to write characters and picking up new words. It helped me focus on something and reengage my mind during my depression. I had no idea how or where I could use the knowledge now that I had been deported from China; I just knew that Chinese would come in handy in my life. After all, as I said before, if life forced me to understand this language, I would not resist. If I set a goal to learn Chinese, I would not give up. I remember my friends saying it was a strange decision, but I didn't listen to them and just kept going toward my goal. Yang and I talked to each other every day and it helped me learn the language much faster.

After a month, my mother was discharged from the hospital and she was feeling a little better. She even started eating and gained a couple of pounds. I was really happy about that. I tried to spend all my time with my family and friends. After all, they needed my attention just as much as I needed their support. I had mood swings from good to bad and back again several times a day. I tried to rest more to maintain balance. I had no idea how I was going to live my life, but I tried not to think about it so I wouldn't feel that confusion. I tried to just be happy that I was alive and home. I was really happy to see my family and friends. Everything else seemed completely unimportant to me.

It turned out that when I was in prison, my father kept a calendar on the wall where he marked each day. Elsa and I spent a total of 192 days in prison. Every holiday, my father wrote me letters of congratulations. I was able to read them with tears in my eyes only after a month. He had found information about similar detentions of Ukrainians in China. He even found other detainees' families and called them, offering moral support and communicating with them all the time. I was shocked to hear all this.

In prison, when we thought we were forgotten and nobody cared about us, all our friends were panicking because we had disappeared. Maybe it's a bad comparison, but I literally saw what would happen if I died. It was like I died and came back to life. I lost everything—my health, my ambitions, my business, and, above all, myself. I remember myself as a different person before prison. I remember everything that happened before as if it wasn't me. I now fully understand the meaning of the phrase "life divided into before and after," because that's exactly what happened to me.

I became a completely different person and it's hard to explain. I felt different about myself. Before I dyed my hair black and had low self-esteem, I was very insecure and didn't think I was beautiful. In prison, when I had to strip naked with unshaven legs in front of crowds of people, I got rid of a lot of these complexes.

In prison, I was used to seeing my body in a horrible state and accepting it, but I didn't see myself in the mirror for half a year. It's really hard. It's like I lost myself and started to appreciate what I had. Then, at the airport, when I saw myself in the mirror for the first time, I decided that I was only going to get better.

After prison, I dyed my hair white. They say being blonde is a state of mind and it's true. I'm still blonde. As it turned out, white hair color suits me very well because I have white skin and blue eyes. It was only after prison that I started to appreciate it.

If it wasn't for prison, I wouldn't be the person I am today. Difficult situations in life break us down or become a point of growth in our personality. But the choice is always ours to give up or move on. For me, it became a point of growth. I have changed both externally and internally. I can't say that I am grateful for this experience—I don't want anyone to go through what we went through—but if it wasn't for prison, I wouldn't now value myself, my appearance, and what I have.

Prison literally raised me and made me an adult. The hardships in my life didn't end in prison. After all, our whole life is a struggle. And we always have a choice: to be strong no matter what or to give up and complain about fate and circumstances. I chose to be strong a long time ago.

I spent three months with my parents. Their health improved and for the winter holidays I decided to go to Poland to visit Elsa. I missed her and her family very much.

Many of our friends asked if our friendship had grown stronger after prison. No one can ever understand us the way we understand each other. I've been asked how often I think about prison. Both Elsa and I would answer every day. Even after six years, we think about it every day. Prison is a part of our lives, a part of our past. It's like a burden that's always with you—you just get used to living with that pain, but it never goes away.

Even after six years, I remember it like it was yesterday. It's hard to live with those memories, but I have no choice. I flew to Poland for the New Year, 2019, as did our Chinese friend, Cao. He didn't know English at all, but he flew to Poland to support us after prison—this is another example of the humanity of the Chinese people. At that time, I was continuing to learn Chinese and could already translate elementary phrases. I spent Christmas vacation with Elsa, her family, Cao, and our friends in Poland. We were happy for the first time in a long time.

I wondered if I could live in Western Europe with them. I stayed in Poland for a couple of months. I even tried to find a job. But it was very difficult without knowing Polish. I continued to learn Chinese and the only person who supported me was my father. Yang invited me to visit him in Hong Kong. I really wanted to see him, so I said yes. He consulted a lawyer who said that Hong Kong was a free zone where I could stay even if I had been deported from China. Yang bought me tickets and I went to the airport in Warsaw, but as soon as I stepped through the airport, I had a panic attack. I felt sick at the thought of having to give my passport to someone. That was the trigger for me. I remember feeling dizzy and panicked. Fear overcame me and I had to run away from the airport. I cried from fear and helplessness. Part of me wanted to go back to Asia, but my fear prevented me from doing so. Yang was already waiting for me in Hong Kong and I had to tell him the truth. He understood me like he always did. He said I just wasn't ready yet. Too little time had passed and I had to wait.

I returned to my family in Ukraine and went on a week-long trip to Europe with my friend. I had to drink strong sedatives before every trip to the airport. We traveled around Europe for a week and I tried to find the answer to whether I could live in Europe. But the answer was already inside me. I didn't see my life in Europe and decided to look for ways to move to Asia.

I remembered the show *Taiwan* that we had watched in prison. I started looking for information on the internet and learned that Taiwan is not part of China. It's an independent state where the official language is Chinese. It turned out that there are many Chinese language schools in Taiwan and many foreigners from all over the world go to Taiwan to learn Chinese. I decided that I needed to go to Taiwan to learn Chinese.

In the spring, I was able to overcome my fear and fly to Hong Kong to see Yang. I was so happy that I could finally speak Chinese with him because he didn't speak English. That's when Yang and I started dating. We decided that I would go to study in Taiwan to be closer to him and would see him often in Hong Kong. I was in love and happy. I think it was the first true love of my life. After everything that had happened to me, falling in love with a Chinese man was the weirdest thing. But love is what energizes us and makes us happy. I felt it for the first time when I was twenty-two. I tried to look at things realistically and didn't understand what to do about it. I just knew I had to get my life together and do something.

It took a couple of months to get a student visa. After that, I traveled to Taiwan for the first time in August 2019. My decision was difficult for my family to accept. Because of the stress I was going through, they were afraid to let me go anywhere, but they just had to accept my decision to go to Asia again—they could not control me.

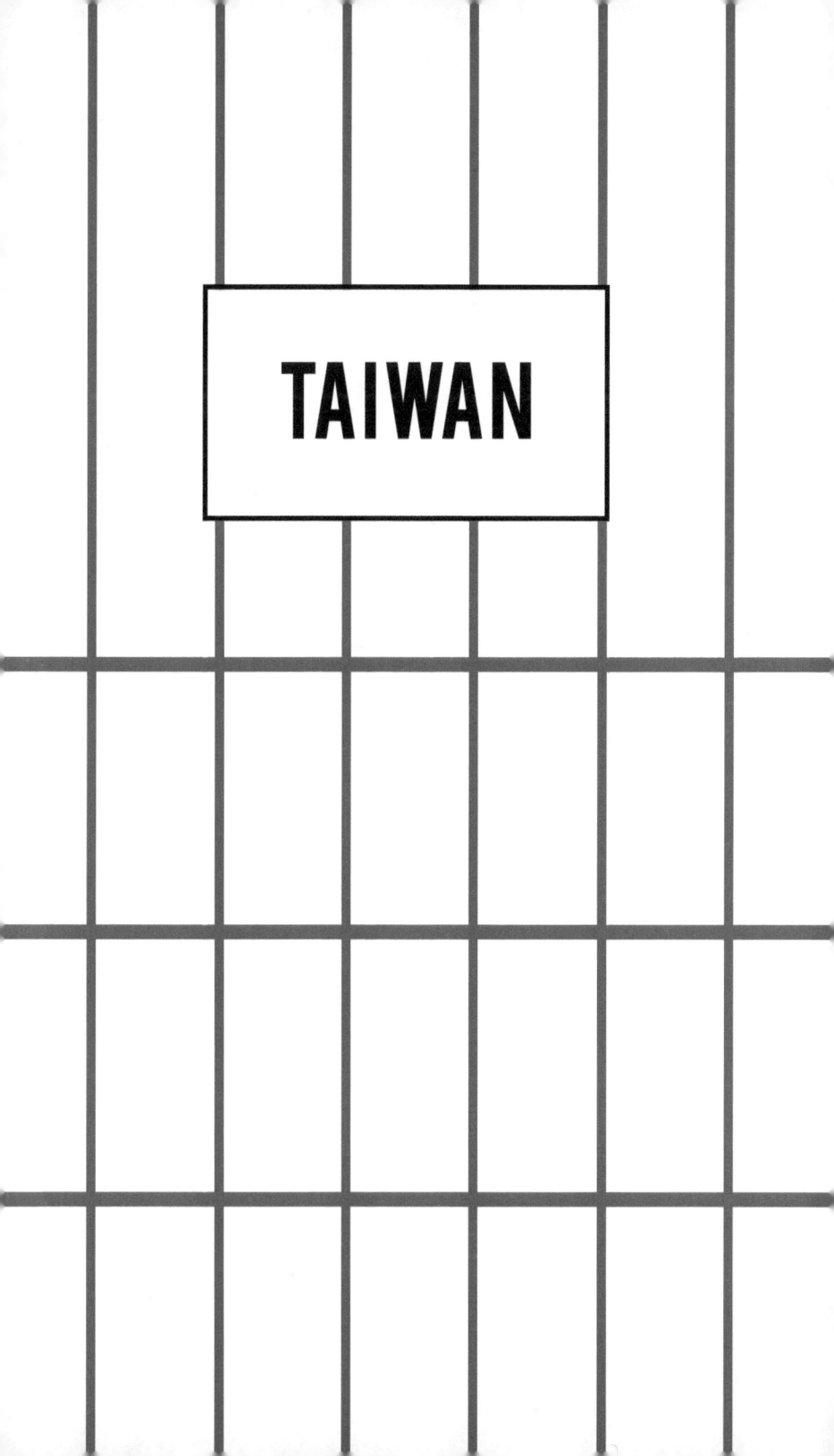

I flew to Taiwan and didn't even know how to get from the airport to the city. I didn't have any friends or acquaintances. I was just happy to see a new country and to be back in Asia.

I rented a hotel room for a few days and went to a language school the next day to take my Chinese language exam. I remember walking down the street on the first day and asking the first man I met where I could buy a SIM card. He was very kind to me and it turned out that he was a realtor. He immediately offered me help in finding an apartment and I accepted.

I didn't expect Taiwanese people to be so different mentally from Chinese people. Taiwanese people are very polite and friendly. They are always happy to help a foreigner on the street. This was a shock for me after my experience in China.

My new acquaintance refused to take money for his services. A day later, we made an appointment to meet at his office. I walked around the neighborhood, looked at all those cozy streets with flowers and lots of restaurants, and thought about how I would like to live there. A couple of days later, my new realtor friend found me an apartment in the same building I had walked around. He even signed a guarantee for me to the owners of the apartment. And so, after five days in a new country, I rented my first apartment.

My landlords turned out to be a nice couple in their sixties. They were as friendly and kind to me as possible. During those five years, they helped me many times. They even took me to the doctor when I got sick. I can safely say that I have been very lucky to have them. Initially, I thought Taiwan was no different from China. But after being here, I learned that Taiwan is a democratic country where everyone has the right to vote and protest, unlike communist China.

Taiwan is also the first country in Asia to allow same-sex marriage. That speaks to the level of tolerance of society as a whole. At first, I experienced culture shock like all foreigners who have come to live in Asia. But the friendliness and openness of Taiwanese people certainly help you adapt to your new environment faster. Taiwan immediately impressed me as a country with an ideal society.

It was hard for me to accept that you could just leave your phone and things on the table in a café and walk out into the street. You could leave your bag open in the night markets and never be afraid that something would be stolen from you. You never had to count your change or worry about being cheated.

I remember the first time a policeman came up to me on the street and asked me if I needed help. Of course, my first reaction was fear because this was a particular trigger for me after prison. It took me a long time to realize that I was safe. I found triggers everywhere. Whether it was police cars, the immigration office, or the walkie-talkies of the restaurant staff, I realized that my unexplainable anxiety attacks were not normal, but I didn't know how to deal with them. I thought they would go away with time.

I was very surprised by the Taiwanese medical system. It was a shock to me that I could go to any doctor late at night without waiting in line. Even if I didn't have insurance, it costed me little money. After living in Ukraine, it was hard for me to realize that such a thing was possible. In fact, most foreigners find it hard to realize, especially in contrast to China. But once you get used to this comfort, it's hard to leave.

Taiwan gave me the impression of a dreamland. I wondered how on one island there could be big cities with tall buildings and millions of inhabitants, all very close to beautiful nature. In the first couple of months of living on the island, I made friends with whom I traveled to different cities and beautiful places. It is impossible to convey the beauty of the oceans, mountains, waterfalls, and small islands in the ocean. It is impossible to convey all the excitement of this country. In those moments, I was truly happy.

It is very hard not to fall in love with Taiwan and its hospitality, atmosphere, beauty, and insanely delicious food. Taiwan even has its own smell, which cannot be confused with any other country. Every time I fly here, I walk out of the airport and smell it.

In Taiwan, they use traditional characters, and I had trouble with that. I had previously learned simplified characters, so I had to learn them all over again. For the first couple of months at the language center, I spent several hours a day learning hieroglyphs. I was a diligent student. However, I was under a lot of stress. I felt inferior to my classmates because I was not the best reader. My mood was constantly changing from joy at having completed my daily assignment to tears and fear that I was failing. It was very hard for me to deal with my low self-esteem and self-criticism, especially after everything I had experienced in China, but I had no choice. I forced myself not to sit still, to study hard and fight fear. I realized that my future depended only on me. I had to be strong and adapt to this country as quickly as possible. I was mainly driven by the fear of going back to Ukraine. That has always motivated me.

Yang and I saw each other often in Hong Kong. One weekend, Elsa even came to visit us. We were scared to be in Hong Kong, and it was especially hard to go through passport control. All the memories from prison haunted us. We had to overcome our fear no matter how hard it was. Yang was very supportive of us morally and that was invaluable.

Yang was my first love and I was insanely happy with him, but our relationship went too far and we had to decide what to do next. I had been deported from China ten years ago. He was Chinese and couldn't visit Taiwan without a visa. He had a serious business in China that he couldn't leave for me. We couldn't see each other all our lives in Hong Kong. So, after five months of my life in Taiwan, we decided to break up because we had no future together. It was a terrible tragedy for me, leaving me alone in Taiwan without any support, another ordeal for me. I felt confused and unwanted. I realized that I was alone on the other side of the world. My friends and family were too far away to help me. I realized that I could only rely on myself.

My financial savings were running out and I had to look for a job. I had no idea what to do. According to Taiwanese law, people from Europe can't work in regular jobs as laborers unless they have special education. I have a Ukrainian lawyer's education and I can't work abroad with it. My goal was to stay in Taiwan, but at that time it seemed impossible to me. My student visa was expiring and my money was not enough to continue paying for my studies.

I started looking for a job and asked everyone I knew. My friends started telling me that with my looks I could work as a model. I never thought of myself as beautiful—how could I model? But I had no other options. I knew I had to find any way I could to stay here. I had to find a way to get a work visa.

I met an agent who was looking for foreigners who spoke Chinese to be on a TV show. It seemed unreal to me at the time. I went to see the filming of this TV show. All those cameras, the lighting, other foreigners who speak so well...I felt like I couldn't be a part of that society. But then I told myself that a year ago, they were all here, and I was in prison and didn't understand a word. If I've come this far, I can't give up. So I said yes, even though I didn't believe I would succeed.

I had to leave the country because my visa was expiring. At the last moment, two days before my flight, the agent and I agreed that I would fly to Ukraine, make a modeling portfolio, and he would apply for a work visa for me. I couldn't even get all my things. I realized all the risks and the complexity of the situation, and I had no choice but to risk everything to stay in the country.

I flew to Ukraine with a connection in Hong Kong. In Hong Kong, I had to leave the airport, spend the night in a hotel, and fly to Germany in the morning. It was very painful for me because I missed Yang. I associated Hong Kong only with him. When I arrived in Hong Kong at passport control, I was sent for questioning. This time they asked me the purpose of my visit. I explained that I was just transferring between planes. With no explanation, I was enclosed for several hours in a room with a cage with other foreigners. They took my passport and my suitcase.

I cried with fear because all this was a strong trigger for me to remember prison. I had absolutely no idea what was going on. Then I was told that I didn't pass through passport control and I had to go back to Taiwan. But my visa to Taiwan had expired. The immigration officers treated me with the utmost disrespect. They yelled at me that I had to pay for the tickets back to Taiwan, even though I had tickets to Germany the next morning. They physically forced me onto a plane and sent me back to Taiwan.

I flew to Taiwan, but my visa had expired. I was met at the airport by Taiwanese immigration officials. They started to calm me down, gave me tea, fed me, and put me in a hostel inside the airport for free. In the morning, I was given free tickets to Germany with the words "You have done nothing wrong, you are always welcome in Taiwan." This is a prime example of how different Taiwanese and Chinese attitudes toward foreigners are. At that moment, I was convinced that I wanted to return to live in Taiwan.

I flew to Ukraine, made a modeling portfolio, and sent it to my agent. While I was waiting for an answer on my visa, I got poisoned and ended up in the hospital. I was in the hospital under IVs with severe food poisoning and had no idea what to do next. All my belongings were in Taiwan and I didn't even know if I could go back.

After a week, my visa was approved and I was able to fly. But due to my health condition, I had to stay in the hospital and missed my flight. My friends and parents supported me. My friends paid for my apartment in Taiwan. When I felt better, my parents gave me the last of their money for a plane ticket. I bought the ticket and went to Taiwan without the slightest idea of how to live, where to work, or what to do next.

On the way to the airport, I cried with fear. I had $50 in my pocket and a couple thousand in debt. This money would be enough for me to eat for a few days. I flew to Taiwan, got my residence permit on a work visa, and started sending my portfolio to all the agencies with the hope of finding some work. I remember that feeling of deep loss and hopelessness. After all, the unknown is very scary. I didn't even have any work experience, but I didn't give up. I agreed to any low-paid shoots to somehow survive and obtain work experience. I felt fear and anxiety all the time. These feelings became permanent for me.

It turned out that my looks were in great demand in Asia. If someone had told me before that I would be a model, I would never have believed it. I wouldn't have even believed that I would dye my hair white. I had to believe in myself and become more confident. As time went on, the work expanded. I could already afford a normal standard of living. I started doing TV shows on local television and my career took off.

For the first couple of years in Taiwan, I suffered from severe depression. At first, I didn't realize I was depressed. I thought I was tired and just worried a lot about work and money. In my opinion, the hardest thing about depression is that people don't realize what is happening to them. That was the case with me. I was constantly forgetting things, and it was hard to cope with everyday routine. Because of the constant stress, my condition only worsened. I had nightmares about prison all the time and I couldn't stop it. I had panic attacks from time to time, but I didn't realize what they were. I just called them bouts of uncontrollable fear. I suffered from post-traumatic stress disorder without knowing it. I had to take sedatives all the time to feel better.

Later, I went to a psychiatrist and was prescribed mild antidepressants and sleeping pills. It was the only way I could live normally. I was glad that I was living in Taiwan, but I had to fight with myself and my fears every day. I remember having a phobia of documents. I couldn't go to government offices such as banks or the migration office because the employees of these institutions were in uniform and I would need to sign documents. Before going to the bank, I had to take sedatives so that I could at least control myself and not cry.

I was very tired mentally of myself and my emotions. But there was nothing I could do. In big restaurants in Taiwan, waiters and managers often use walkie-talkies to transmit information between them. Hearing a voice on the walkie-talkie once was enough to make me feel scared and nauseous. I would immediately remember prison and how scared I was to hear the sound of a walkie-talkie in the hallway. Such memories followed me everywhere and I couldn't stop them.

Every time I encountered one of these triggers, I would relive the stress all over again. For the first couple of years, my condition steadily got worse and antidepressants didn't help much. I realized that I needed professional help. I couldn't live like this anymore. I couldn't control myself and it was really bothering me. I couldn't plan anything because I couldn't foresee my condition. It made it very difficult to work.

At some point, I decided to start seeing a therapist, and it was the best decision of my life. I wish I had done it right after prison. Antidepressants only take away the symptoms of depression for a while, whereas a psychotherapist and working on yourself can help you cope with the problem at its core.

Psychotherapy is difficult, expensive, and takes time and effort. It's daily work. It's perfectly normal to be unable to cope with stress on our own. It is normal to be overwhelmed by a wave of emotions we can't control. All people have the right to be weak. There is no shame in seeking help from loved ones or doctors. After all, it is only with the help and support of others that we can survive the most difficult events. Stress always has a negative impact on our physical health. It seems to me that this is the main reason we should keep an eye on our mental health.

In my experience, I noticed a certain pattern. During times when I was experiencing depression, I was constantly sick with various minor illnesses. When I felt mentally better, my physical health also got better. During these couple of years of constant worry and depression, I started having problems with my insulin production. The nervous system directly affects the onset and development of all diseases. For me, this was another reason to monitor my mental health and seek help from a therapist right away.

I have always been a fairly social person. I have had a lot of friends since childhood. I have always been a sincere and open-minded person. It has never been difficult for me to share my experiences with my friends. In a new country, I made new friends with ease. But even I faced the problem of social isolation. For the first three or four years of my life in Taiwan, I could not tell my friends about my prison experience. It never hurt me to talk about it or remember it because it was part of my life, but it was hard for me because I was afraid of judgment. I was afraid that someone might think I was lying about why I went to prison. After all, being in one of the most brutal prisons in the world because of visa problems sounds a bit absurd and unbelievable. This difficult experience affected my personal relationships as well.

I thought I wasn't worthy of having a normal relationship because I was inferior to other people. If I had any personal relationships with men, they were short-lived. I always kept my distance. I preferred not to talk about my past and never talked about prison. I didn't really talk much about myself. I was also afraid of being judged by the man I liked. It was easier for me to keep quiet and remain aloof. It's very difficult to live with these beliefs. It affects your self-esteem first and foremost.

It's hard to live when you feel inferior to other people. Self-esteem affects work productivity, ambitions, social life, and how we feel about ourselves in social society. These beliefs are always at the subconscious level of a person and it is impossible to change them independently. Only psychotherapy can help one cope with this. It took me about two years of psychotherapy to be able to tell my new friends about my experience. I was a little surprised that they didn't question the reason for my detention. They didn't think the way I did. I basically made up my own problems. No one ever judged me. On the contrary, they said that I am a strong person and not everyone can survive something like this. But I always joke and say that I could not just lie down and die.

In prison, I was made to believe that I was a criminal. That belief kept me from living my life for a very long time.

I truly feel sorry for people who have gone through similar experiences. I feel sorry because I know how hard it is to get back to a normal life. I always tell everyone I know that if you have experienced something like this, don't be afraid to seek help. If I could help people who have been through similar experiences, I would advise them to seek psychological help.

Now you know how a person who has experienced incarceration feels. If someone close to you has had a similar experience, they may be withdrawn because they need help and support from others.

I know for a fact that prison is a turning point in every person's life. It is impossible to come back from prison the same way. Prison changes our personality whether we want it to or not. Prison breaks our life and divides it into before and after. Once you've been through it, you can never go back to normal. You can literally ruin your life by harboring misdirected beliefs and low self-esteem. But it can make you stronger. We always have a choice and it can be our point of growth. It can be a reason to become a better person or to start life over. The most important thing is to work on yourself and your thinking.

Prison is part of my life and I am used to it, but I still cry when someone tells me that someone they know is in prison. I can't even watch movies that involve prison in the plot. I immediately think of all the heartache, fear, and hopelessness Elsa and I felt when we were there. The least I can do is tell people about my experience. I have been asked many times by friends if I could go back in time and change things. Would I change that situation? I always say no. Because then I wouldn't be who I am now. The experience has made me much stronger, more confident, and probably smarter. It helped me mature at an early age. But at the same time, I would never wish that on anyone.

I believe that my story is not a story of success. My life is not perfect and there are many things I want to change. However, my story *is* about never giving up and always believing in yourself first and foremost. It's more of an example of an eternal struggle, whether with circumstances or with yourself.

Taiwan has really become my home. I travel around the world a lot and I can't imagine my life in any other country. I love Taiwan because this is where I was accepted as a full member of society; this is where the years of my youth were spent. I love Taiwan for the comfort, the mentality of the people, the attitude toward foreigners, and the delicious food. I come back here like it is home every time. My heart belongs to this island.

I've lived in Taiwan for five years. One day, I realized that I was living the life of my dreams. I work as a model, actress, and TV host. I earn enough to travel the world and live the life I want. I speak fluent Chinese and have many friends. Even though I don't consider it the pinnacle of success, my story is an example of never giving up. Before, I couldn't believe it was possible either. In prison, I didn't believe the suffering would end. After prison, I didn't believe I could handle the depression. Then I didn't believe I could live in this beautiful country. For a while, I couldn't believe I could deal with my fears. But everything passes and all difficulties end sooner or later.

We can always do more than we think. We have to realize that our whole life is a struggle. Our life is very unfair. You have to accept that. The most important thing is always to believe in yourself and your future. After all, our future depends only on us.

Elsa and I live on different islands in different parts of the world, but we are still close and understand each other like no one else. We communicate every day and often travel together. I am lucky to have a best friend. If I had to go through such a difficult experience, I am glad it was with my best friend.

In Taiwan, there is always the threat of war with China. I may have to move to another country and learn another language someday, but no matter what happens, I know that I have me and I can handle everything.

# ABOUT ATMOSPHERE PRESS

Founded in 2015, Atmosphere Press was built on the principles of Honesty, Transparency, Professionalism, Kindness, and Making Your Book Awesome. As an ethical and author-friendly hybrid press, we stay true to that founding mission today.

If you're a reader, enter our giveaway for a free book here:

SCAN TO ENTER
BOOK GIVEAWAY

If you're a writer, submit your manuscript for consideration here:

SCAN TO SUBMIT
MANUSCRIPT

And always feel free to visit Atmosphere Press and our authors online at atmospherepress.com. See you there soon!

# ABOUT THE AUTHOR

I'm **ANN LIN**. I was born in a Ukrainian village in 1997 in a family of rural workers. I studied at the best university in my country and should have had a good future. But because of the problems in my country, I had to grow up early and leave home at the age of 20. I have traveled a difficult path, which I have described in this book. My life has always been full of contrasts: difficulties and moments of happiness, good people and disappointments, successes and failures. But my main secret is that I have never given up. My story has a happy ending. And I hope that my example can help others to overcome difficulties on their way.

www.ingramcontent.com/pod-product-compliance
Lightning Source LLC
LaVergne TN
LVHW041629070526
838199LV00052B/3287